D1535386

THE BLUE-FLY
IN HIS HEAD

THE BLUE-FLY
IN HIS HEAD

POEMS

BY JOHN HEATH-STUBBS

LONDON
OXFORD UNIVERSITY PRESS
NEW YORK   TORONTO
1962

Oxford University Press, Amen House, London E.C.4

GLASGOW NEW YORK TORONTO MELBOURNE WELLINGTON
BOMBAY CALCUTTA MADRAS KARACHI LAHORE DACCA
CAPE TOWN SALISBURY NAIROBI IBADAN ACCRA
KUALA LUMPUR HONG KONG

PRINTED IN GREAT BRITAIN

CONTENTS

ACKNOWLEDGEMENTS

SOME of these poems have appeared in the following English periodicals: the *Times Literary Supplement*, *The London Magazine*, *Outposts*, *Stand*, *Satis*, *X*, *The Fortnightly*, *Frontier*, *Poetry and Audience*; and in the United States in *The National Review*, *Arbor*, *Generation*, *Audience*.

The Cave of the Nymphs

HUSHED, haunted the cave—a gathering point
For time and eternity. One entrance
For men, subject to death,
One, open to the sky,
For the Undying. In this place,
Where the quiet nymphs weave purple cloth,
And hive the learnèd bees—archetypes,
Images, symbols.

But Ulysses,
Ulysses of the many stratagems,
Was unaware of this. He shook himself (grandson
of Autolycus, the wolf-man) suddenly awake
Like a great canine. He rubbed the salt from his eyes,
Dismissing the images of night and journeying:
The snatching horror, the sucking whirlpool,
Canticle of the death-birds,
Possessive and beast-attended
Goddesses, the geometrical gardens.
He knew where he was. The landscape
Was not the deceptive pastoral simplicity
Of the cannibals' island, and not
The hothouse vegetation of Lotos-land,
Nor spruce and silver-birch
Of the Laestrygones' fjord. It was limestone;
It was tamarisks; it was olives
And vine-stocks gnawed by goats.
It was Ithaca at last. And was dangerous.

Therefore, out in the sunlight,
Meeting a shepherd-boy,
He started once more to lie—
It was almost routine with him now—

Improvising a cover-story. But with so much blague,
And such a ready tongue,
He began to enjoy it. And that other,
Knowing it would all come out,
Could not refrain from revealing herself—
the goddess who was on his side—
And chaffed him too. So they stood there,
The man and the Immortal, like a pair of friends
Who understand each other
Too well to talk much.

And as he turned to go
She still smiled after him. But if
The perdurable and inviolate heart
Of immortal Wisdom might grieve, it ached then
For what it could never know:
For not to know death is to know nothing
Of the wonder of deliverance; and to be free
Of the wide aether, and the white peaks of Olympos,
And all the bounds of the world and the backward-flowing Ocean,
Is never to know and love
One patch of earth as home.

But Ulysses,
Ulysses who had made a good journey,
Was unaware of this. He had gone to look for
A wife he had not met
For twenty years, and a son
Who must now be a stranger to him.
For he had come home;
Which is the whole point of the story.

Not being Oedipus

NOT being Oedipus he did not question the Sphinx
Nor allow it to question him. He thought it expedient
To make friends and try to influence it.
In this he entirely succeeded,

And continued his journey to Thebes. The abominable thing
Now tame as a kitten (though he was not unaware
That its destructive claws were merely sheathed)
Lolloped along beside him—

To the consternation of the Reception Committee.
It posed a nice problem: he had certainly overcome
But not destroyed the creature—was he or was he not
Entitled to the hand of the Princess

Dowager Jocasta? Not being Oedipus
He saw it as a problem too. For frankly he was not
By natural instinct at all attracted to her.
The question was soon solved—

Solved itself, you might say; for while they argued
The hungry Sphinx, which had not been fed all day,
Sneaked off unobserved, penetrated the royal apartments,
And softly consumed the lady.

So he ascended the important throne of Cadmus,
Beginning a distinguished and uneventful reign.
Celibate, he had nothing to fear from ambitious sons;
Although he was lonely at nights,

With only the Sphinx, curled up upon his eiderdown.
Its body exuded a sort of unearthly warmth
(Though in fact cold-blooded) but its capacity
For affection was strictly limited.

Granted, after his death it was inconsolable,
And froze into its own stone effigy
Upon his tomb. But this was self-love, really—
It felt it had failed in its mission.

While Thebes, by common consent of the people, adopted
His extremely liberal and reasonable constitution,
Which should have enshrined his name—but not being Oedipus,
It vanished from history, as from legend.

Theseus on Naxos

I

MOTHER seldom spoke of Father:
   She'd a faded photograph—
Tall and rather worried figure
   With a great carved oaken staff

(Am I looking somewhat like him
   Now I've got my worries too?)—
That, and a few withered violets
   Which had once been vivid, blue.

These she kept between the pages
   Of—oh, I forget the name—
Odes and Dithyrambs—or something—
   By some modish Lesbian dame.

Darling mother's taste in verses!
   Still, I'm not the one to judge—
What you'd call a man of action;
   Most poetic stuff is fudge.

'Violets, these, from Cecrops' city
   Where your father reigns', she said,
When I coaxed her to display them
   (To delay the time for bed).

Not a wholly normal childhood,
   Being—well, 'the fruit of sin'—
Or, to put it bluntly, bastard
   (*And* my school-chums rubbed it in).

Then I got 'his' sword and sandals—
   Time the local boy made good—
(Mother said she *wasn't* crying)—
   Ventured through the Dangerous Wood.

5

How I there eliminated
  Various anti-social types
Frequently has been related—
  Kites and crows enjoy their tripes!

(Take, for instance, that Procrustes
  With his calculating eyes,
Who stretched travellers out, or cut them
  Down, to fit his standard size:

In his way a true idealist—
  Never thought it was enormity—
Man a thing to be transcended
  In that Higher Uniformity.)

Thence to violet-crownéd Athens:
  Touching scene with dear old Dad;
Took me two weeks to discover
  That the place was really bad.

First, a rather passée sorceress
  Had poor father on a string;
I was forced to send her packing,
  Borne aloft on dragon's wing—

Whirled on high in a fiery chariot,
  Queen of the Night in a four-wheeled star,
Dragon-drawn, and trilling curses
  Through empty spaces where no gods are.

Then the Cretan tribute, stifling
  As it came by year, by year,
Streets of that white-paven city
  With a pale, unspoken fear:

Delicate girls in the blush of beauty,
  Boys in their galloping grace, to the Beast—
Product of hideous and comic lust:
  The obscene guzzle, the bull-thing's feast.

II

Aegean-dandled island of Crete:
  Before I dreamed it, I had come,
Voluntary victim, to liberate
  Athens, I now knew was home—
  Suddenly, inexplicably, home.

Corridored palace of Knossos,
  Throne-room of Minos the king,
The bull-games painted, the double axe,
  And young girls dance in a ring—
  Bell-skirts, bare breasts, in a ring;

Eyes of Minos, thalassocrat,
  Lord of the bull-voiced wave,
Who must make up accounts with God
  At the ninth year's end in a cave—
  Is it birth or death in that cave?

And the staring eyes of a girl—
  Adriadne's, that king's daughter—
Bird-eyes that seemed to burn with delight
  (Was it of love or slaughter?)
  On me, destined to slaughter.

Secretly she came that night
  (She had bribed the guards, as I guessed)
To the close dark hell of a man in fear,
  And I lay upon her breast.
  And I dreamed of my mother's breast.

She gave me a thin-spun cord;
  I held it, and walked in a daze
Threading the echoing corridors
  Of a hollow, haunted maze—
  Of the palace, or of the maze.

Princess, or priestess, or goddess,
    It was the ritual task
She had assigned me; I killed
    A bull—or behind that mask
    The king, in a bull's mask?

I do not know; We fled
    Through darkness where snickered no star,
Over shaggy seas to Naxos:

            ★   ★   ★   ★   ★

That's precisely where we are.

III

All the time I think of Athens,
    Athens which will now be free:
People needing laws and justice—
    And that business lies with me.

God knows, what can I do for them?
    But it's not for me to choose;
Father will not live for ever;
    I must step into his shoes.

Ariadne, with your witchcraft,
    Life, and all, I owe to you;
But, as queen of civic Athens—
    Really, it would never do.

Ariadne, mountain priestess,
    Wild-eyed enthusiast
Of swift-footed Britomartis . . .
    I shall live to weep the past.

8

Dearest, you were very gentle—
   Delicate and white those hands;
May the strange gods whom you worship
   Guard you on these wind-vexed sands.

Look, how peacefully she's sleeping!
   Dark now; it will soon be day.
Quietly set the sails and leave her—
   Surely it's the kindest way.

Plato and the Waters of the Flood

In one of the remoter parts of Asia Minor, near what was once the southern boundary of the Phrygians, there is a warm spring flanked by a Hittite monument, and known to the Turks as Plato's Spring. The reason for the name is that it was at this spot, according to Arab legend, that Plato succeeded in stopping the Flood by making the waters run underground.

W. K. C. GUTHRIE, *Orpheus and Greek Religion.*

WHEN on Armenian Ararat
   Or Parnassus ridge
Scrunched the overloaded keel,
   Pelican, ostrich,
Toad, rabbit, and pangolin—
   All the beasts of the field—
Scrambled out to possess once more
   Their cleansed and desolate world,
         Plato, by that fountain,
           Spoke to the swirling deep:
       'Retire, you waters of Chaos,
         Flow retrograde, and sleep;
      Above the swift revolving heavens
        Rule the intelligible,
       Chaste and undecaying ideas;
        Brackish waters, fall!'

Plato, in the academic grove,
   Among the nightingales,
Expounded to wide-eyed ephebes
   His geometric rules;
Reared a republic in the mind
   Where only noble lies

Reign; he expelled the poets
(With courtesy, with praise).
                Loaded with useless garlands,
                    Down to that fountain
                The exiled poets proceeded:
                    'When will you rise again,
                Ten-horned, seven-headed seraphim,
                    Out of your abyss,
                Against the beautiful Republic—
                    Nor tamed by Plato's kiss?'

Titus and Berenice

'TURN to me in the darkness,
　　Asia with your cool
Gardens beyond the desert,
　　Your clear, frog-haunted pool;
I seek your reassurance—
　　Forget, as I would forget,
Your holy city cast down, the Temple
　　That still I desecrate.'
'*Buzz!*' *said the blue-fly in his head.*

'In darkness master me,
　　Rome with your seven hills,
Roads, rhetorical aqueducts,
　　And ravaging eagles;
Worlds are at bitter odds, yet we
　　Can find our love at least—
Not expedient to the Senate,
　　Abominable to the priest.'
'*Buzz!*' *said the blue-fly in his head.*

Titus the clement Emperor
　　And she of Herod's house
Slobbered and clawed each other
　　Like creatures of the stews;
Lay together, then lay apart
　　And knew they had not subdued—
She the insect in his brain,
　　Nor he her angry God.

NOTE. *According to a Jewish tradition Titus was afflicted with an insect in his brain as a punishment for his destruction of the Temple.*

The Peacock and the Snake

'IT was your fault! It was your fault!' cried the Peacock.
'And it was yours too,' whispered the Snake.

'It was lust! It was lust!' shouted the Peacock.
'Yes, and pride, and vanity,'—so the Snake.

'I loved him! I loved him!' shrieked the Peacock.
'And she was sweet, sweet,' hissed the Snake.

'I look at my feet and I scream'—the Peacock.
'And I have no feet'—the Snake.

'It was your fault!' 'Yours also perhaps?'—thus the Peacock-
    Angel
And the diabolical Snake down in the filthiest pot-hole

Where they exist, reproached each other,
Timeless in their torment. But somewhere

Within the innocent jungle, the peacock (which is a bird)
Displayed beneath the bough a fragment of God's splendour;

And the coiled snake (which is a reptile)
Deployed upon the ground a portion of His subtlety.

In Every Sense of the Word

W<small>HEN</small> my heart was young I wasted my body
In every sense of the word Love

Now my body is older I waste my heart
In every sense of the word Love

My mind and my spirit reproach me both
In every sense of the word Love

There will come a wind and disperse all four
In every sense of the word Love

They will meet again on the Judgement Day
In every sense of the word Love

For Heaven can burn, and Hell can burn
In every sense of the word Love

Judgement Judgement Judgement Judgement
In every sense of the word Love

My heart will grieve, my body will groan
In every sense of the word Love

My mind too late will repent, and my spirit—
In every sense of the word Love

My blue cold spirit will still be free
In every sense of the word Love

In Hell to burn, in Heaven to burn
In every sense of the word Love

14

Bert and the Seven Deadly Sins

BERT
Never showed that he was hurt,
On his side:
That was Pride.

He continued to term her 'his Silver Chalice':
That was Malice.

While reacting like a bull to a red cloth:
That was Wrath.

And regretting what, in his stupidity,
He wasted on her: that was Cupidity.

The situation continued—both
Were guilty of Sloth.

But, in middle age, discovered refuges—
Love's febrifuges—
Drink, drugs, a good dinner, the weed:
That was Greed.

Yet he still loved her, for her bitchery:
That was Lechery.

So they were damned,
And into Hell crammed
(After they died)—
Where she became his bride,

To torment him with other Furies:
Decision of celestial juries?

The Ballad of Don and Dave and Di

DON and Dave and Di—

Dave
Was an artist (no man's slave);
But Don
Always got on;
And Di
Was anybody's apple-pie.

Don loved Dave, and Dave
Loved Don
(I wonder why)
And both loved Di,
But Di
Looked after Di.

Di married Dave
(God save
The mark, she thought he'd save
Her from her inner lie.)

But Don
Got on, got on,
And off with Di.
She saw the point of pie
Not in the sky.

Dave hated Don,
But he forgave
(I wonder why).

But Don could crave
No hatred then for Dave:
Don still had Di,
And he caressed her thigh.

Said Dave:
'One of us three must die;
And if it's Don
I'm bound to sigh
Over his early grave;
And if it's Di
I know I'll cry.'

Don still had Di.
She was his slave.
Till, by and by,

Don killed Dave
(I wonder why).
It was an unmarked grave.

Don still had Di,
He still got on.
Till Di
Drove him to an early grave.
(God knows why.)

Johnny Appleseed

JOHNNY Appleseed wherever he went
From just-round-the-corner to the Firmament
Planted apple-trees; and they were bent.

The graft they came from was all right
Till a married couple, against the light,
Forewent their lease at one bite.

Johnny was mixed up in that affair,
Disguised as a grass-snake, though Regent of the Air—
But his own account is, that is not fair:

He is not interested in Original Sin;
Which is something we have got under our skin,
And he never supposes he can win.

He thrust a seed deep in maternal Nature's
Heart, and distorted her virginal features:
All creatures are unkind to all other creatures.

He flung a fruit in the face of the Goddess of Art,
Who had some connection with the human heart,
And definitely upset *her* applecart.

Involved also the scientific technique,
Which had been invented by an ancient Greek:
Pride, prejudice, stupidity are not far to seek

Meddled also with the political animal,
Therefore each party programme seems so small
And you hate to vote conservative labour or liberal.

In short, effected the whole Universe:
Which is partly why this is such bad verse—
You can't push a ball-point but under a curse.

I think that for the destruction of Man
He hung a split seed in the sky of Japan,
Which we do not seem to be able to ban.

I am telling this story with the lid off:
I do not know how we can get rid of
Johnny Appleseed. But instead of

Hereby invoking the concept of Grace
(Which can hit you like a slap in the face,
And transform, leaving scarcely a trace,

Or in the mode of a still, small voice
Continually advocate a definite choice—
A situation which is not nice)

I recommend merely we should take heed
Not to cultivate that weed; nor breed
The apple-seed of Johnny Appleseed.

Household Devils

PIPES don't draw, gas-fires pop,
Sinks get choked, chains won't pull,
Milk turns sour in steamy kitchens,
Cigarette-lighters burst into flames—

Possessed by the little household devils
That grimace at me from recalcitrant objects.

Towards human beings I generally exercise
Reasonable forbearance and charity
(Being the way they are):
A sneak has picked my heart from my pocket—
I bring myself to forgive him.

But *they* more frequently and effectively
Trip my heels into mortal sins
Of rage and blasphemy.

Seven in particular sit on the typewriter
Transforming it into a fiendish device
For mangling communication
It gnashes its 42 teeth.

So I approach it with the understandable
Reluctance of the male spider
Approaching the female spider
To be chewed up in the act of love.

Articles don't get written,
Poems don't get copied;
The grime of sloth settles on my life.

They remind me also if I only traded
(Like practically everyone else)
My soul and my talent for a little gold
I might after all be graciously living
In easier and sleazier circumstances
Among gadgets and gimmicks which actually work.

Use of Personal Pronouns:
A Lesson in English Grammar

I

I is at the centre of the lyric poem,
And only there not arrogant.

'You begin every sentence with *I*'—the rebuke was well taken:
But how on earth else am I to begin them?

You and Thou

You are a secret *thou*.
Fumbling amongst the devalued currency
Of 'dear' and 'darling' and 'my love'
I do not dare to employ it—

Not even in a poem, not even
If I were a Quaker, any more.

Beginning as an honorific, the unaffectionate *you*,
For English speakers, has put *thou* out of business.
So, in our intimate moments,
We are dumb, in a castle of reserve.

And He alone
From Whom no secrets are hid, to Whom
All hearts be open,
Can be a public *Thou*.

He, She, and It

Only in the third person sex raises its
Unattractive—well, 'head' is a fair enough euphemism.
The thought of sex in which you and I
Do not participate is (unless we are *voyeurs*)
Either horrifying or ridiculous. He and she
He it and she it.

But, moving outside the human order,
We observe there is no personality
Apart from gender. Animals are *it*,
But our own cats, horses, and dogs are *he* or *she*;
The huntsman's Puss is *she*, Reynard is *he*;
And even ships are beloved as *she*,
Cars and bicycles, even.

For the homosexual queening it in the Gimcrack Bar
His colleagues, objects of his scandal, are *she*,
While the inaccessible youth in the tight jeans,
Three buttons undone in his scarlet shirt,
Is, however, an *it*.

One

One thinks of *one* as a pronoun employed principally
At Cambridge, modestly to include oneself
And other people in one's own set,
At Cambridge. One appreciates the French usage
Of *on*; one knows one's Henry James;
One does feel (or, of course, alternatively, one does not)
One must, on the whole, concur with Dr. Leavis
(or, of course, alternatively, with Mr. Rylands).
At Oxford, on the other hand,
One tends to become *we*. At Cambridge
One senses a certain arrogance in the Oxford *we*;
A certain exclusiveness in the Cambridge *one*
Is suspected, at Oxford.

We

'We', said Queen Victoria, 'are not amused.'
Subsuming the entire dinner-table into the impersonal
And royal *We*:
No wonder the effect was devastating.

We is also the Editor of *The Times*
While a Greek chorus is a pattern of dancing *I's*;
The Christian congregation is *I* in the Creed,
Thou in each of the sacraments,
Otherwise solidly *we*. And
'Let Us make man in Our own image.'

We is not amused, nor is it interested
In the possibilities of defeat.

They

They is the hellish enemy of paranoiacs
(And even of Auden and Edward Lear);
They is in a conspiracy, is directing hostile thought-waves,—
Has got everything fixed *their* way. *They* will not let you.

History a deadly and unending struggle
Of class and national *theys*, except when sometimes
An imperial and oecumenical *We* serenely
Frowns at a barbarian and utter *they*.

But for you and I
Weeping in our tragic citadel, the horror
Is simply to realize that *they* exist.

Footnote on Epic Diction

ACHILLES let slip a wingéd word:
Beowulf word-hoard unlocked;
Homer knew, Widsith and Cædmon knew,
Words are not expendable.

For the quick Greek the musical, bee-like creatures
Hiving between the wickerwork of his ribs
In patience confected the honey of his eloquence;
But an errant swarm is no profit.

And the slow Saxon in the dragon's cave of his breast
Concealed the troll-worked and elaborate gold;
Churlish and unthrift not to keep it dark—
It could carry a curse.

But with us the air is pestilent with words,
Loud speakers perambulate the market-place:
The counterfeit penny that cheats and corrupts,
Winged motes that buzz and sting.

Egypt, 1956

Ars Poetica

I

ONE thing *imprimis* I would have you remember:
Your poetry is no good
Unless it move the heart. And the human heart,
The heart which you must move,
Is corrupt, depraved, and desperately wicked.

Milton denoted poetry
'Simple, sensuous and passionate'.
But who has said, my dear,
Human sensuality and human passion
Were ever simple matters?

But poetry is not 'emotional truth'.
The emotions have much less to do with the business
Than is commonly supposed. No more than the intellect.
The intellect shapes, the emotions feed the poem,
Whose roots are in the senses, whose flower is imagination.

Call it then: 'A humane science'
(Like all science concerned
With a world that really exists)—but humane:
Beatrice could request, not command Virgil—
She among the blessed, and he in Limbo—
He can take you as far as the Earthly Paradise
But no further than that.

In Limbo also is the Master of them that know:
But he is a Master. Therefore respect critics,
Especially the uncomfortable ones.

But there is no field of any activity
In which the parable of the wheat and the tares
Is more applicable.

The poem does not propound
Your or anyone else's opinions,
However admirable, however fascinating;
With luck it may touch the skirts
Of universal Wisdom.

And much the same goes for the passions:
The oaf in love *may* be a poet
Or bumpkin tongue-tied still;
A poet in love may be no less oafish.
And so in eloquence remember
All things exist in Love.

I mentioned just now luck—our Lady Fortune
('Bright-haired daughter of Chaos' I once called her)
She also is an exalted goddess,
Germane to the Muse. Therefore revere her.

II

A poem is built out of words;
And words are not your property.
They are common counters, involved
In private chaffering, and international transactions;
They have been tossed into the caps of beggars, and plonked
On the reception-desks of brothels.

In your case they are the English language:
Not the Greek flute, nor the Roman trumpet,
Nor the Welsh harp, nor the Spanish guitar,
Nor the French clavecin,
But a sound bourgeois piano
Capable of something of each.

You have got to make language say
What it has not said before;
Otherwise why bother—after a millenium,
(And a bit more) of English poetry—and you a wren
Rising from the eagle's back?

Work against language. It is your enemy.
Engage in a bout with it.
But like a Japanese wrestler
You will overcome by not resisting.

III

The words come to you from the commercial districts:
From the shop-bench, and from working in the fields;
But contrary to much of the practice of the age
There is something to be said for politely requesting them
To wipe the mud off their boots
Before they tread on your carpet
(Supposing you own one).

And if they should emerge from the reading-room
Tactfully suggest they remove the cheese-parings,
Dead flies and biscuit-crumbs from among their whiskers.

I have no personal objection
If you want to put on singing robes:
At a ritual you don't wear work-a-day clothes.
But the surplice and chasuble, or the Geneva gown
Are nothing more than the Sunday best
Of a Byzantine gentleman, or a Renaissance scholar;
And any clergyman, I suppose, would look pretty silly
If he walked down the street in them.

So under existing social conditions
You had better think over this matter of your costume
With a certain perspicacity.

IV

A poem is like an iceberg:
Seven-tenths under water
(And what is below the surface—
This may at first have seemed—
To you the most important.)

Like an iceberg—cold, hard,
Jagged and chaste, glittering
With prismatic colours, as it drifts
On unpredictable deep-sea tides. Against it also
The titanic folly of the age
May shatter itself as it goes through its joyless night.

V

'Patience and perseverance
Made a bishop in his reverance.'
The proverb ought to have added
'And the charisma of the Holy Ghost.'

Mutatis mutandis
(And it is very much *mutandis*)
This likewise is relevant.

So through patience, perseverance, luck and that sort of thing
(I can only wish you luck)
You may arrive at an actual poem—
An interjected remark
At a party which has been going on
For quite a time (and will, we trust, continue);
A party at which you are not
A specially favoured guest
And which you will have to leave before it is over.

Let us hope the others will occasionally recall it.

But to you it will seem a little world.
You will look at your creation and see that it is good.
In this you will be mistaken:
You are not, after all, God.

THE sun is eclipsed; and one by one
The birds stop singing—
Folded their wings:

But I never heard
That the frogs stopped croaking.

On Reading an Anthology of
Japanese Poetry

'*Rather old manastic query pond*
Hopfrog jumpskip in
Splishersplosher.'

—And it was either the frogs or probably the insects
(A lineage more antique) perfected
And taught the Japanese this art of *haiku.*

Grasshoppers, metallic beetles, dragon-flies, mantises—
Do they not continually meditate and exchange
Among themselves little poems like this?

'*Petal to twig recurs—*
Correction—butterfly.'

In Japan highest world-incidence of myopia
(Their vile script and vitamin-deficiency);
Nowadays they are all goggle-eyed with glasses
Which, combined with their buck-teeth,
Reinforces the insect connotation.

A chain of unproductive overpopulated
Inclement islands. A religion
Forbidding the taking of life
(Economy largely based on fisheries)
Forbidding violence
(A history of feuding samurai).

And if of a man hanging by his teeth
One inquires 'What is Zen . . . ?'

The moment of absolute intuition,
Contemplation of snow-flurries and plum-blossoms,
Has not made them noticeably more moral:
Nor us our morality.

'Fresh grasses of summer—
Relic of heroic dreams?'

May-Fly

UNDER the willow whose roots are shallow
The dismissed lover laid his head down,
       And down, and down:
  May-fly, May-fly, living a day,
  It was good while it lasted—even gay?

Under the oak which storm-winds broke
The defeated general laid his head down,
       And down, and down:
  May-fly, May-fly, dead in an hour,
  What then is glory, what precisely is power?

Under the elm, the treacherous elm,
Whose boughs can break, the ruined businessman,
For his country's sake, laid his head down,
       And down, and down:
  May-fly, May-fly, grub in a stream
  Eating dirt, for years eating filth—for a dream.

Under the fire of the sweet-briar
The fading beauty laid her head down,
       And down, and down:
  Bridal May-flies thick in the haze—
  Once and once only! Praise! Praise!

Under crossed boughs the unfrocked priest
Laid his head down—'I have been a beast!'—
       And down, and down:
  Finished May-flies falling to death—
  God is spirit, spirit is breath.

Under the laurel in continual quarrel
The obscure poet laid his head down,
And down, and down:
Dead May-flies on the waters strewn,
And dead words are drifted on.

Lament for the 'Old Swan', Notting Hill Gate

THE Old Swan has gone. They have widened the road.
A year ago they closed her, and she stood,
The neighbouring houses pulled down, suddenly revealed
In all her touching pretentiousness
Of turret and Gothic pinnacle, like
A stupid and ugly old woman
Unexpectedly struck to dignity by bereavement.

And now she has vanished. The gap elicits
A guarded sentiment. Enough bad poets
Have romanticized beer and pubs,
And those for whom the gimcrack enchantments
Of engraved glass, mahogany, plants in pots,
Were all laid out to please, are fugitives, doubtless,
Nightly self-immersed in a fake splendour.

Yet a Public House perhaps makes manifest also
The hidden City; implies its laws
Of tolerance, hierarchy, exchange.
Friends I remember there, enemies, acquaintances,
Some drabs and drunks, some bores and boors, and many
Indifferent and decent people. They will drink elsewhere.
Anonymous, it harboured
The dreadful, innocent martyrs
Of megalopolis—Christie or Heath.

Now that's finished with. And all the wide
And sober roads of the world walk sensibly onwards
Into the featureless future. But the white swans
That dipped and swam in each great lucid mirror
Remain in the mind only, remain as a lost symbol.

Bryant Park, New York

ADJACENT to the Public Library, not far from the public lavatory,
A rectangle, paved; and with trees, and with green—

From an altiloquent and alien beauty
Nostalgically I turn into this enclave

(It recalls London.) I wish they kept it better:
Rain-soggy newspapers; and a few not old

Not young men sit and stare here;
They are slumped behind illegible eyes.

Mine meet instead those of the bust erected
By the Goethe Society of America,

Eyes which equally are turned to stone
(Needed no sculptor to accomplish that),

Pleased to encounter a European acquaintance
(With respect; with, one hopes, humility)

Though personally I have not much liked Goethe—
Tempted to think that he deserves this place?

The Prison of St. Louis, Mansura

THEY gave him the judge's house,
The best house in the town—a fine and airy cage
For a royal bird to mew in. The spy-hole
Is pierced in the roof (tactful) where the guards stood,
And the squalid cupboard under the stairs
Was apparently for his chaplain, who, I hope,
Was a monk and a holy man, and had a vocation,
Or at least, was habituated to such quarters.
For courteous they were, and, anyway,
There was money to be had for this, the Christian king.

Only one touch they added—
The door through which he daily had to pass
To take, under surveillance, exercise
Is barely four feet high. So, he must stoop,
Who was taller by a head than any of his knights,
And, for a ransom, would not beggar France.

—(For clear-eyed France, self-violated now,
Playing the harlot under every green tree
On the Algerian hills!)—

          Blessed Saint Louis,
That our personal freedom shall not
Be based on the ruin of others, and in the hour
Of our humiliation, pray for us.

1957

Zante

THEN from the pangs of the Aegean storm we burst,
The crystals of the weather formed once more
Around the sun's gold seeds. And, naked as
That green-haired century of Nereus' daughters,
Promontories and islands in procession
Breasting the sea's clear vintage. So for days
The far-shot arrows of a god beat down
On grey of rock, green-grey of olive-leaves,
Blue-green and dazzle of moving waters; so that the heart
Stands still, and the brain aches, and the eye falters.

The centaur is standing just behind the hill:
The pipes are, but for a moment, hushed.

Aeolian and Ionian names . . . And now, Zante,
To starboard rising—but not voiceless,
Island of poets and exiles!—You, Foscolo,
And you, Kalvos, whom the east wind of freedom
Swept to that holy city of the Celts
Where I go home; but now recall
The Cyprus gaols, the gallows and the guns—and I
Cannot without shame, cannot without tears
Honour this beauty.

1957

NOTE. *The poets Ugo Foscolo (1778–1827) and Andreas Kalvos (1796–1869) were natives of the Ionian island of Zante. Both became Liberal refugees in England. The phrase 'the holy city of the Celts' is applied to London in a poem by Kalvos.*

The Parthenon

WHERE they tamed the wild Libyan
Unmarried war-goddess, goatskin-aproned;
Transmuted the owl-shrieking bugaboo
Into an image of Wisdom—

A dash in a reckless and exorbitant taxi
Will get you there; then climb
Above the esurient, lively, and stuffy city,
Feet slipping on loose stones.

Suddenly it stands there; like a familiar quotation
From dusty oleographs, the model
Of every second-rate 'classical' building—
Church or museum—

Off-white like a sea-worn shell,
Like a bird's skull,
Under remorseless light;
Denuded the colour and gold

Long since; the centaurs and heroes
Shanghaied to Bloomsbury.
It seems very small:
And She has departed.

So that's all. There is nothing to do
But stand and gape like any other
Romantic tourist; and then go.

But turn your back, and stumble
Down the steep track—then suddenly
The mathematical candour,
Neither over- nor under-statement,

Owl-clawed, hooks to the heart.

The Sphinx

IT is not feminine: this crouching cat-beast
Kneading a vacant temple between its claws—
Napoleon and the rest
Can fire their guns in its face. In the vicinity
Of the pyramidical Pyramids, where the lanner
Nested, and boys can easily scale,
For a few piastres, an old cove's tombstone,
It will stay, it will gaze
At the rising, rising sun, until the sun
Forgets to rise, and Time ruins, and it, too,
Crumbles—the implacable image
Of male power that smoothly worships itself.

From the Spanish of Juan Ramon Jimenez

AT the side of my dead body
My work lives on.

The day
Of my life fulfilled
In nothingness and in all things—
The flower that is closed with the opened flower;—
The day of contentment in departure,
Through contentment in remaining—
In remaining through departure; the day
Of pleasant sleep, knowing it so, for ever,
Sleep ineffable and maternal
Of the empty rind and the dry cocoon,
At the side of the eternal fruit
And the infinite butterfly.

To Edmund Blunden

on his 60th Birthday

THYRSIS, or Meliboeus, or old Damoetas—
I must address you
By some such green, Virgilian-vowelled name—
You, the last and truly-tempered voice
Of all our lovely, dead, and pastoral England:
The radio brings that voice to me tonight,
Reading your poem, the vocables
With Kentish loam adhering to them still.
You on the Chinese shore, and I
In Alexandrian garboils? No—
For fourteen years are abrogated now;
The evening sun is gilding Abingdon,
And Kirk White's verse, and Bloomfield's, and Clare's
Our topic as we sit here at the bar,
And brown-haired boys are playing in the street.

1957

42

News from Egypt

Taken from Juvenal's Fifteenth Satire

EVERYONE knows what they worship in Egypt—a country gone
    haywire—
Monstrosities. One district bows down to the crocodile,
In another they stand in awe
Of the ibis because it eats snakes. The golden graven
Fetish of a sacred monkey glisters
Where the enchanted arpeggios sound and resound
From the fractured torso of Memnon and Thebes
Lies ancient, and hundred-gated, and ruined. The cat and the
    catfish—
These are their gods; whole townships
Are given up to the dog-cult—hunting-hounds, but never
The Goddess who is their patroness. It is taboo
To masticate onions and leeks (Oh holy people
Whose deities sprout in the garden!) taboo
On mutton for dinner, or anything else that bears wool;
Taboo on the seethed kid—but cannibalism?
That is entirely in order. When Ulysses
Spun this sort of yarn over the supper-table
Alcinous was thunderstruck; maybe his audience laughed,
Maybe they just lost patience—that clearly unreliable
Anecdotalist. 'What, is there no one
Will chuck the man in the creek?—He's certainly asked for it—
To get a horrid and real acquaintance
With his own whirlpool-demon—inventing such stuff,
His man-eating ogres and one-eyed cannibal giants.
I'd sooner believe in
The sea-bitch snatching, the blue rocks clashing,
The skin-full of storm-winds,
And Circe with one delicate touch of her wand
Transmogrifying Elpenor and those who rowed in his galley
Into a snorting drove of porkers.

43

Does he think us Phaeacians as vacuous-pated as this?'
That's what anyone present might have remarked,
Who was not yet drunk, who had tippled but lightly
Out of his native wine-cask. The man from Ithaca—
Well, it was his story, and he was the sole authority.

★　★　★　★　★

There are two villages, Ombi and Dendera, neighbours.
Between them burns an old, old feud; malice
Which never dies, and wounds that will not heal:
Because, particularly, each place detests
The other's gods, supposing
The ones they have themselves the only genuine article.
So, when the one held a fête-day
It seemed an occasion too good to be missed to the others—
Their village elders and headmen—to spoil the fun,
Put paid to their feasting,
With tables spread at each temple and each crossway
And benches day-long and night-long set out
For a whole week on end. Egypt is crude enough—
I know all about that—but the riff-raff,
When it comes to extravagant luxury, doesn't give way to
Any notorious sea-port town of the delta!
It looked like a walk-over, over sozzled men,
Staggering and burbling in their wine. On one side
Fellows who danced to the strains of a negro piper,
Flowers on their heads, and garlands,
And some sort of hair-oil. And on the other
Devouring hatred. A prelude of abuse—
A trumpet-signal to their inflamed minds. Then both sides,
Shouting, rush together. Bare hands savaged
In place of weapons. Few cheeks without a gash,
And scarcely a nose or none came out of that fracas
Which wasn't broken. Through all the ranks
Battered faces, features disfigured, bones
Showing through ripped-up cheeks, and fists

44

Dripping with blood from eyeballs. But this
Was only playing at fighting, they thought, and kids' stuff—
No corpses to kick around. For what's the good
Of having a mob of so many thousand rioters
If everyone stays alive? They pick up stones from the ground,
Weapons of civil faction,
And twist their biceps to throw them. Not such boulders
As Turnus hurled or Ajax, nor that with which
Diomede smote Aeneas on the hip; but such
As unheroic hands may cast, those of our modern age.
Our race was degenerate
Even in Homer's days. Now earth brings forth
Humanity as evil as it's puny.
Whatever God looks down laughs at and loathes it.

But to get back to our story where we left off. One side
With reinforcements now, draws knives, augments
The fight with thick-showered arrows.
The others, who inhabit
Neighbouring Dendera with its shady palm-groves
Quickly turn tail under the Omoite charge. But one,
Who's in too much of a hurry with panic,
Slips in his tracks and is caught. Now the victorious mob
Hack up his body into bits and pieces,
So that one dead man could be enough to go round,
And eat him all, down to the gnawed bones:
Not broiled in a brass kettle, not roasted on a spit—
How slow and boring, they thought, to wait for a fire,
Being entirely content with a raw cadaver.

*　*　*　*　*

What drove these men to this—extremity of famine,
The rigours of a siege? What impelled them
Into this shocking atrocity? If the Egyptian earth
Itself ran dry, what more could they wish to do
To shame the tardy-rising Nile-flood? For never
The frightful Nordics, nor the British Islanders,

45

Nor murderous nomads of the steppe, nor monstrous
Transylvanian hordes raged as these raged—
This cowardly and good-for-nothing canaille,
Who hoist toy sails on cockle-shells of ships,
And with their tiny oars
Ply painted china boats. What punishment
Could one think up for this, what tortures
Fit for these people to whose twisted minds
Hunger and rage are one? Nature proclaimed
Man's utmost tenderness of heart when she endowed
The gift of tears; our noblest faculty—
Compassion. Therefore she decrees
We grieve to see a friend in trouble in the law-courts,
In all that degradation, or when a boy still under age,
Whose tear-stained face and girlish hair
Appear almost ambiguous, is forced to bring
A fraudulent trustee before the bar. Under her jurisdiction
We sigh meeting the bier that's borne along
Of a young unmarried girl, dead in her bloom, or when the earth
Closes over a baby's body, one
Too young to be cremated. For what righteous man,
Worthy to bear the torch in the sacred Mysteries,
Or such as Ceres' priest would have him be, believes himself
Alien from other's sorrows? For this alone
Separates us from the dumb brutes; and through this same
A spirit to be honoured is apportioned to us,
Fitted for things worthy of gods, and fitting
To learn and put in practice knowledge, and thereby
We have drawn down from heavenly citadels
Feelings, denied to the beasts that grovel. At the world's beginning
That which established all things gave to them
Merely the vital principle, but to us Mind. So that with us,
A mutual charity demands that each
Shall seek and proffer help; demands to gather
The scattered individuals
Into society; demands migration

From the primeval forest, leaving behind
The jungle where our ancestors lived: and we build houses for
    ourselves,
With another's roof close by our own privacy,
So that, through the nearness
Of a neighbour's threshold, the sense of trust
Which comes from being together
Gives us to sleep secure. We defend with arms
Our fellow-townsman fallen, or maybe,
Faltering with a grave wound; sound forth to battle
One trumpet summoning all, and are protected
By the self-same fortifications, and behind gates
A single key may close.

★   ★   ★   ★   ★

FIRST STEPS IN
PHYSIOLOGUS

A little bestiary for beginners

THE PIG

NOT improved by domestication. Wallows
In its own filth. Screams
As loud at feeding-time
As when it is killed—throat slit,
Hung up by the heels, the blood
Drip-dripping out of it.

Omnivorous, adaptable—like us;
He has secured a good Second
In Evolution. He is cunning—
You cannot fence him in—
But the ring in his nose is no badge of honour.

The pig has much the same idea
Of sensuality as you have. Scratch his back,
With your hand (if you don't mind),
With a stick (if you are particular),
He will pay you in grunts. He is the hero
Of so many of our sagas
(From Curly Wee to George Orwell); and ought to have been
A wild boar rushing out of the Ardennes,
All tusks and bristles, the crest
Of our thundering Saxon ancestors
And of the last
(And possibly maligned) Plantagenet.

But has no tragedy now—unless a flood
Overtakes him: then he swims
Until he cuts his throat (in a combination
Of fat and despair) with his little, bifid hooves,
Which will never play Bach, or paint a picture.

WOULD rather run up-hill than down-hill;
Would rather look backwards than forwards;
Escapes by going the long way round,
Or by lying still.

Mad? A wild lover,
And a bouncing prize-fighter;
But, a careful mother,
In tussocks of couch-grass
Abandons her leverets.

Wounded, captured, screams
Horribly, like a child;
Is eaten half-putrid, boiled
In its own dark blood;

And is sacred to the Moon,
A type of innocent sacrifice.

ALWAYS to be at home
For the tortoise may be as burdensome
As for the human being,
His continuing exile:

The foxes have hide-outs,
The birds of the air their cradles—
They are free to come and go:
To the tortoise, his dome.

'Stroking, a waste of time,'
(Said Sydney Smith) 'You might as well think,
Caressing St. Paul's, to please
The dean and Chapter.'

                But was wrong,
For he is sensitive,
Even to the roof-tops;
Vegetarian, inoffensive, longaeval,
Condemned, through seven generations
Of men, to trundle
The load of his home-keeping.

THE GECKO

(For J. P.)

I DON'T know how many thousand years
Of evolution have not taught the gecko
You can't jump *up* downwards.

Blue-flecked, pink-flecked, semi-transparent,
Sucker-footed, he creeps
Across the ceiling. He sees
With his extraordinary protuberant eyes
A fly, just hovering below him . . . He

                    jumps
                        and

Flick!
      He falls to the floor:
Poor little half-dazed lizard!

How did this absurd, this innocent creature
Become a symbol of evil?

The Copts say:
'Saint Shenouda commanded us to destroy you!'
Whereat the thing is supposed to curl up and die,
Or at least depart, embarrassed.

And everyone, Moslem or Christian, is agreed
It sneaks into houses, it spits
Into the salt-box, tabernacle of life,
Contagious of leprosy;
Like its own whiteness it fades to in the dark.

Shenouda, intransigently holy father,
Striding out of the desert with grit in your beard,
Do you concern yourself, then,
With such trivialities?

It could be so. In your day,
In those of Pachomius, Anthony,
The wastelands pullulated with dragons.
This is a parody, a miniature.

There is so much evil in the world
Anything can be a symbol of it.

The starling is my darling, although
I don't much approve of its
Habits. Proletarian bird,
Nesting in holes and corners, making a mess,
And sometimes dropping its eggs
Just any old where—on the front lawn, for instance.

It thinks it can sing too. In springtime
They are on every rooftop, or high bough,
Or telegraph pole, blithering away
Discords, with clichés picked up
From the other melodists.

But go to Trafalgar Square,
And stand, about sundown, on the steps of St. Martin's;
Mark then, in the air,
The starlings, before they roost, at their evolutions—
Scores of starlings, wheeling,
Streaming and twisting, the whole murmuration
Turning like one bird: an image
Realized, of the City.

LESS bird than voice,
Than the ghost of a voice of a bird,
Of a ghost-bird—moth-owl, fern-owl,
Twilight's great moth-winged, moth-pursuing swallow,
Bark-mottled invisible squatter—Oh why,
Walking now through the garish streets
Of London's noisy midnight, recall this?—
The nightjars each to each, at their churning and spinning,
Over the New Forest heath—
(Years ago now: dwindled the air's gold)—
And soft death-rattle of a pleasing day.

THE CHOUGH

At the London Zoo

So you've got King Arthur's soul inside you, have you?
You certainly look it, gazing
Over your aristocratic, arched, and vintage
Coral bill. Your nostrils
Are covered with soft plumes, and not with bristles
Like the crows with which you are usually classified.
Sundeval, I know, that square-headed Swede,
Put you in the phalanx *Humilinares*,
Or 'humble-nostrils,' amongst a flock of starlings.
I trust you regret that. '*Ay-ow, ay-ow*' you cry
With an accent indistinguishable from
The jackdaws which replace you. You are no longer
Cornish; you are barely Welsh, or Manx.
You are in mourning for something.
For you, like others, palpably must
Become extinct, unless kept in a cage.

AN APOLOGY TO THE FISH

I APOLOGIZE to the fish (or fishes)
Because there is not much about them
In this series, sequence, collocation or whatever
Of verse, prose, poetry or whatever.

Anyway, I think fish have been fairly well dealt with
By others I would not wish to emulate
And would be embarrassed to have excelled—

Such as Leigh Hunt, Rupert Brooke, &c.
(And I've not forgotten Diaper, Mr. Grigson.)

To tell the truth, I'm not very good on fish:
A goggle-eyed, cool, un-talkative, elegant people—
The royal, small-mouthed sturgeon: the mackerel,
Pure as a cirrhus sky,
Feeding on corruption; the carp
That does not flinch when the Japanese eat him alive;
The pike, pickerel, perch, tench, roach, and so on;
The trout, the salmon-trout, and the salmon—
They are so much alike and I forget how to classify them.

Perhaps there are more poetic possibilities
In the invertebrata—the octopus,
Sacred to the Goddess, and subject to nervous breakdowns;

The starfish with five bodies and one head; the sponge,
Which draws in through its pores and respires through its
        mouth,
And is both a city and an individual;

And the sea-anemone—
The carnivorous flower, the sucking rose of the sea.

THE LOCUST

IT is only a grasshopper, after all:
I had a good look at one once
In Alexandria, as it climbed up a wall
In the hot, hot Egyptian autumn—the same great eyes,
The grave and horsey face, and the angular,
Arched and leaping shanks.

Some Russian or other
(I forget the name) has proved it—innocuous grasshoppers
Mutate, in the starved lands
(Incompetently or greedily farmed
Till they are desert). So, locusts are created,
A sign of judgement,
And no green thing withstands.

So here it is, climbing up a wall
In the hot, hot autumn; a straggler from its army,
Bearing in itself the prophecy
Of Abaddon's abominable hoards—
The scorpion-tailed, the woman-tressed, the kingly-crowned
Troop, that will occupy us.

THE ANTS

You could have been human, but you aren't.

CICADAS of Greece—persistent
Chirr chirr chirr—unambiguous, almost harsh
(Rock off-white, glaucous leaves,
Sun-beat Aegean splendour).

The voice of poetry, this, in the ear of Socrates;
It takes its dram of dew; it is loved
By the slim-ankled maids of Piera.

       ★   ★   ★   ★   ★

The American model is different:
Begins, jaunty on tree-tops,
To whirr like a tiny, delicate dynamo;
But soon stops.

THE BED BUG

THE bed bug is like Cain
A wanderer on the face of the earth—
Perpetual immigrant,
Being an intimate lover of Man;
An exiguous Count Dracula.

By nature he is sub-tropical:
He likes warm places—snug
As a bug in a rug.

His name, I fancy, is originally Arabic
(He returned with us from the Crusades)
But 'contaminated', as philologists say,
With Anglo-Saxon *bug*—'goblin' or 'devil'
(Cf. Slavonic *Bog* = 'God').

I have been eaten by bed bugs
In three continents so far:
Those in the Parisian Latin Quarter
Were certainly the worst
(They had had Villon and Verlaine before).

A ruthless spraying of DDT,
Burning sulphur, arsenical smoke-bombs
Will get rid of bed bugs. But the natives
Generally seem to prefer to be bitten
Until they become immune from the irritation.

Or you can simply learn to sleep with the light on:
The bug is afraid of light.
But this is to take a rather Manichaean attitude—
Exchange of blood with any of God's creatures

Is (as of course John Donne knew)
A matter with serious implications.
It has something to do with love.

America has a variety
Known as the 'kissing bug' . . .

NOTE. *This insect is placed by entomologists as a close relative of those described in the preceding poem.*

THE TWO FLIES

Or 'Windows'

THE fly inside says,
  'I see unattainable
Sky—sublime azure!—
  It exists?' The fly outside,
She says, 'He does not love me!'

NOTE. *The subject 'Windows' for a poem in the* waka *form
(31 syllables) was given by his Imperial Majesty the Emperor of Japan for the annual Japanese Poetry festival
of 1959.*

BANG Bang Bang
Said the nails in the Ark.

It's getting rather dark
Said the nails in the Ark.

For the rain is coming down
Said the nails in the Ark.

And you're all like to drown
Said the nails in the Ark.

Dark and black as sin
Said the nails in the Ark.

So won't you all come in
Said the nails in the Ark.

But only two by two
Said the nails in the Ark.

So they came in two by two,
The elephant, the kangaroo,
And the gnu,
And the little tiny shrew.

Then the birds
Flocked in like wingéd words:
Two racket-tailed motmots, two macaws,
Two nuthatches and two
Little bright robins.

And the reptiles: the gila monster, the slow-worm,
The green mamba, the cottonmouth and the alligator—
All squirmed in;
And after a very lengthy walk,
Two giant Galapagos tortoises.

And the insects in their hierarchies:
A queen ant, a king ant, a queen wasp, a king wasp,
A queen bee, a king bee,
And all the beetles, bugs, and mosquitoes,
Cascaded in like glittering, murmurous jewels.

But the fish had their wish;
For the rain came down.
People began to drown:
The wicked, the rich—
They gasped out bubbles of pure gold,
Which exhalations
Rose to the constellations.

So for forty days and forty nights
They were on the waste of waters
In those cramped quarters.
It was very dark, damp and lonely.
There was nothing to see, but only
The rain which continued to drop.
It did not stop.

So Noah sent forth a Raven. The raven said 'Kark!
I will not go back to the Ark.'
The raven was footloose,
He fed on the bodies of the rich—
Rich with vitamins and goo.
They had become bloated,
And everywhere they floated.
The raven's heart was black,
He did not come back.
It was not a nice thing to do:

Which is why the raven is a token of wrath,
And creaks like a rusty gate
When he crosses your path; and Fate
Will grant you no luck that day:
The raven is fey:
You were meant to have a scare.
Fortunately in England
The raven is rather rare.

Then Noah sent forth a dove
She did not want to rove.
She longed for her love—
The other turtle dove—
(For her no other dove!)
She brought back a twig from an olive-tree.
There is no more beautiful tree
Anywhere on the earth,
Even when it comes to birth
From six weeks under the sea.

She did not want to rove.
She wanted to take her rest,
And to build herself a nest
All in the olive grove.
She wanted to make love.
She thought that was the best.

The dove was not a rover;
So they knew that the rain was over.
Noah and his wife got out
(They had become rather stout)
And Japhet, Ham, and Shem.
(The same could be said of them.)
They looked up at the sky.
The earth was becoming dry.

Then the animals came ashore—
There were more of them than before:
There were two dogs and a litter of puppies;
There were a tom-cat and two tib-cats
And two litters of kittens—cats
Do not obey regulations;
And, as you might expect,
A quantity of rabbits.

God put a rainbow in the sky.
They wondered what it was for.
There had never been a rainbow before.
The rainbow was a sign;
It looked like a neon sign—
Seven colours arched in the skies:
What should it publicize?
They looked up with wondering eyes.

It advertises Mercy
Said the nails in the Ark.

Mercy Mercy Mercy
Said the nails in the Ark.

Our God is merciful
Said the nails in the Ark.

Merciful and gracious
Bang Bang Bang Bang.

PRINTED IN GREAT BRITAIN
AT THE UNIVERSITY PRESS, OXFORD
BY VIVIAN RIDLER
PRINTER TO THE UNIVERSITY